FURTHER FREAKY FABLES

Further FREAKY FABLES

J.B. HANDELSMAN

A METHUEN PAPERBACK

A METHUEN PAPERBACK

First published in Great Britain in 1986
by Methuen London Ltd
11 New Fetter Lane, London EC4P 4EE

This collection © 1986 J.B. Handelsman

Printed and bound in Great Britain by
Redwood Burn Limited
Trowbridge, Wiltshire

British Library Cataloguing in Publication Data

Handelsman, J.B.
  Further freaky fables.
  I. Title
  741.5′942   PN6738.F/

  ISBN 0–413–42270–4

CONTENTS

These Freaky Fables originally appeared in *Punch*
and are published here by kind permission
of the editor and proprietors.

BATHING ONE DAY IN

THE SILENT POOL

AT SHERE, A FAIR DAMSEL WAS SURPRISED BY A GANG OF RUFFIANLY ARISTOCRATS...

ONE OF LANGTON'S ECCLESIASTICAL DUTIES WAS TO VISIT PRIORIES.

THE SHOCK OF SEEING HER HOPELESSLY UNCONSUMMATED LOVER AGAIN WAS TOO MUCH FOR THE EX-DAMSEL, WHO DIED AT ONCE OF AN UNBROKEN HEART.

MORAL: Unfulfilled love is ☐ better than nothing. ☐ nothing. (check one.)

MORAL: Romance language is no substitute for the real thing.

Les Mesdames Sans-Gêne

AS A YOUNG OFFICER, BUONAPARTE TRIED TO JOIN THE CORSICAN LIBERATION FRONT...

MORAL: Waterloo takes many forms.

9

Prologue to Leadership

THE EGYPTIANS WERE GRIEVED BECAUSE THE CHILDREN OF ISRAEL SEEMED TO THRIVE ON ADVERSITY.

See that? I got it building the Sphinx.

Now if you'll excuse us, me and the Mrs have to go and multiply for a bit.

Enough already! Did I not give orders for you midwives to slay the baby Hebrews?

They are too fast for us, Your Pharaocity!

Jumping out of the womb before you can say "Abu Simbel".

Phew! Another day, another pyramid. Where are you taking our son?

Hence.

PHARAOH'S DAUGHTER FOUND THE CHILD IN HIS FLOATING CRADLE, AND…

An Israelite baby! Does um want nefertiti? Someone fetch me a wet-nurse.

THE ACTUAL MOTHER RECEIVED WAGES FOR NURSING THE CHILD, BUT…

I just happen to have this bosomful of milk, you see, Princess.

How I wish I were common and could do such things!

"Amenhotep" is so trite. I shall call him "Moses".

MOSES GREW UP WITH AN IDENTITY PROBLEM, SO…

Behold, my mummy is Egyptian, as mummies so often are, and yet I have this overpowering desire for chopped liver.

An Egyptian smiting a Hebrew! Which one do I identify with? The underdog, I think.

Take that, dog of an underdog!

You should get a cholera.

HE SLEW THE EGYPTIAN, BUT THEN…

A Hebrew smiting a Hebrew! Naughty!

Look who's here, Mr Death Wish himself.

Make it two choleras.

MOSES PRUDENTLY WITHDREW TO THE LAND OF MIDIAN, WHERE…

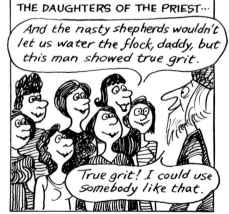

HE INGRATIATED HIMSELF WITH THE DAUGHTERS OF THE PRIEST…

And the nasty shepherds wouldn't let us water the flock, daddy, but this man showed true grit.

True grit! I could use somebody like that.

… WHO LET HIM KEEP ONE. BUT SOON GOD MADE HIM AN EVEN MORE SPLENDID OFFER.

It's Me, in the burning bush! I want you to lead the children of Israel out of Egypt.

But I am unworthy.

Of course you are.

Look at your hand. Leprosy! Look again. Cured! Any time you need a miracle, just call on old **I AM**.

You got yourself a deal, **I AM**.

MORAL: Be adopted.

The Pearl Fishers

of Ceylon assemble to choose a king.

VOTE FOR ZURGA

THE PLEDGE OF CHASTITY

SHE IS THEN ESCORTED BY THE HIGH PRIEST TO THE TEMPLE OF BRAHMA.

BUT LEILA HAS NO SOONER STARTED TO WORSHIP THAN SHE IS JOINED BY HER WORSHIPPER.

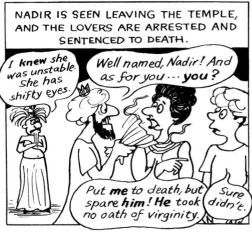

NADIR IS SEEN LEAVING THE TEMPLE, AND THE LOVERS ARE ARRESTED AND SENTENCED TO DEATH.

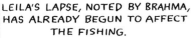

LEILA'S LAPSE, NOTED BY BRAHMA, HAS ALREADY BEGUN TO AFFECT THE FISHING.

MORAL: Do not be a swine before casting for pearls.

the Bees of Ballyvourney

In an excess of zeal, St Patrick had driven the bees out of Ireland along with the snakes.

MORAL: Put honey in thy purse.

Evangeline

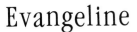

FRENCH SETTLERS IN ACADIA INCITED THE CHIPPEWA* TO ASSIST THEM IN THEIR STRUGGLE AGAINST THE BRITISH.

* or the Cree or the Iroquois or the Algonquin

MEANWHILE, IN LONDON, KING GEORGE WAS LISTENING TO "WATER MUSIC".

Truly divine, Handel! It stimulates the bladder. Yes, Prime Minister?

Your Majesty, there are too many Scots in Scotland.

Send a few to Acadia and rename it "Georgia".

There are already two of those.

"Nova Scotia" then. It has a nice smoked-salmon sound.

His Majesty is evicting the lot of you! We are repopulating the province with a better class of inhabitants.

Surely not better.

Different, perhaps.

Ils sont fous ces anglais! I call it genocide.

I call it gentrification! Those Scots will pay through the nose.

But we French have bigger noses.*

* AT THIS JUNCTURE WE WISH TO APOLOGISE FOR THE RACIALISM OF THE FRENCH.

THE PREVIOUS DAY, EVANGELINE (A MAIDEN OF SEVENTEEN SUMMERS) HAD CELEBRATED HER BETROTHAL TO GABRIEL (AGE UNCERTAIN).

To have and to hold...

To pull and to push...

BUT IN THE CONFUSION OF BANISHMENT, THE LOVERS WERE SEPARATED.

Gabriel! Mon cher financé! The idiot has gone off with his father.

Sorry, Evangeline.

THEN BEGAN HER LONG SEARCH. FLOATING DOWN THE MISSISSIPPI ON A RAFT...

Ahoy the Huck Finn! Seen anything of Gabriel?

Nope, ma'am.

...ARRIVING TOO LATE IN LOUISIANA...

Mon fils vient de partir! Il va à Détroit, qui veut dire—

I know what it stinking veut dire.

...AND IN MICHIGAN. EVENTUALLY SHE CAME TO PHILADELPHIA, AND JOINED THE SISTERS OF MERCY.

Who are you, old man dying of the plague in an almshouse?

I am Gabriel, your one and only.

THEY WERE BURIED SIDE BY SIDE.

And the dowry?

Wait right here. I'll run and get it.

EVANGELINE CREVETTE

GABRIEL LANGOUSTE

MORAL: Once you have found him, never let him go without a receipt.

A Passage from India

Deep in a forest, in a ruined temple, dwelt the beautiful Lakmé with her father, a violently nationalistic Brahmin priest.

THE PLEA WAS PROCESSED THROUGH THE USUAL CHANNELS.

ONE DAY, AS LAKMÉ WAS SINGING IRRESISTIBLY IN THE GARDEN, AN ENGLISH OFFICER BURST THROUGH THE BAMBOO FENCE.

NEXT DAY, DISGUISED AS BEGGARS, FATHER AND DAUGHTER VISITED A MARKET.

LAKMÉ REMOVED HER WOUNDED LOVER TO A HUT IN THE FOREST, WHERE HIS CONVALESCENCE PROCEEDED APACE.

ONE DAY, THERE APPEARED ANOTHER REPRESENTATIVE OF THE BRITISH RAJ.

MORAL: Not to the gods.

THEY HAD HOPED FOR A MALE HEIR; THEREFORE THE DISAPPOINTED PARENTS OF ATALANTA ABANDONED HER ON A HILLSIDE TO BE SUCKLED BY ANY PASSING MAMMAL (SUCH AS A BEAR).

Why do **wolves** always think they're so great?

And I grew up a virgin huntress and the ancient world's swiftest person.

Hey! You aren't supposed to outrun a rabbit.

ANOTHER SET OF INADEQUATE PARENTS, THE KING AND QUEEN OF CALYDON, HAD OFFENDED ARTEMIS (AS EVERYONE DOES); IN REPRISAL, SHE SENT THEM

The Calydonian Bore.

Of a' the airts the wind can blaw, I much prefer the whatsit...

FAMOUS HEROES OF MYTHOLOGY WERE INVITED TO HUNT THE BORE. THEY WERE WELCOMED BY MELEAGER, THE KING'S SON (OR ANYWAY THE QUEEN'S; HIS PATERNITY WAS IN QUESTION).

Theseus — super to see you! Jason, found any good fleece lately? By Gemini, it's Castor and Thing — and ah, the chaste but fleet Atalanta...

Chaste **because** fleet, actually.

O Mary, at thy window be...

We refuse to hunt in company with a woman.

Do you feel **threatened** by this lovely creature?

Hard feta.

In a sense.

Ye flowery banks o' bonnie Doon...

TWO OF THE GUESTS, WHO HAPPENED TO BE CENTAURS, ATTEMPTED TO RAVISH ATALANTA.

So! First blood is human, or equine?

Porcine.

Wee, sleekit, cowrin', tim'rous beastie...

AT LAST MELEAGER SLEW THE BEAST.

There's not a bonnie bird that sings, but minds me o' my Atalanta.

Wha will be a traitor knave?

Me, that's wha.

ATALANTA'S FATHER WAS BELATEDLY PROUD.

And so he presented the pelt to you? How nice! Time for you to get married.

Father, any suitor for my hand must beat me in a foot race, or die.

Certainly, my dear.

A YOUTH NAMED MELANION TRICKED ATALANTA BY DROPPING GOLDEN APPLES AS THEY RACED.

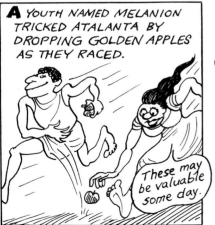

These may be valuable some day.

SHE LOST AND HAD TO MARRY HIM.

A fool who drops apples!

A fool who picks them up!

BUT SHE HAD ALREADY BORNE MELEAGER A CHILD, WHOM SHE EXPOSED ON A HILLSIDE.

O whistle an' I'll come to ye, my lad.

But—

Aren't you and I getting a bit old for this?

MORAL: The apple does not fall far from the tree.

15

TANTALUS,

king of Argos or Lydia, was on intimate terms with the Olympians.

ONE EVENING HE INVITED THE GODS TO A BANQUET.

THE IMMORTAL GUESTS ASSEMBLED.

A SUDDEN OUTCRY FROM DEMETER:

ON ANOTHER OCCASION, TANTALUS HAD PARTICIPATED IN THE THEFT OF A GOLDEN MASTIFF FROM OLYMPUS.

FOLLOWING HIS EXECUTION FOR THESE WRONGDOINGS, TANTALUS WAS SUBJECTED TO ETERNAL TANTALISATION.

A HAPPY OUTCOME FOR PELOPS: ZEUS HAD HIM PUT TOGETHER.

MORAL: There can be no equality, upstairs-downstairswise.

Billy Budd
or, The S·speech Imp·p·pediment

CAPTAIN VERE, LONG RETIRED, GAZED OUT TO SEA RECALLING HIS DAYS AS COMMANDER OF H.M.S. *INTOLERABLE*.

Did I do the wight thing? It was back in '98, no, I tell a lie, it was '97...

...and sevewal new wecwuits had just been dwagged on board.

All impwessed, I imagine?

Oh, t-t-terribly, sir.

I like that young sailor's forthwight though faintly idiotic appwoach.

Well, **I** don't like the stuttering pinhead! His lack of depravity nauseates me.

I'll destroy him or my name's not Master-at-Arms Claggart, and it is.

Squeak, I want you to steal Budd's tobacco.

Why?

Is this mutiny, Squeak? We are at war! Nick that backy!

Attention, men! The weason I am standing here so wesplendently is to induce you to dwive the Fwench fwom the seas.

We will!

H-h-hurrah!

♪ For he's a lovely-looking captain...

B-b-b-m-m-m-t-t-t...

For shame, Squeak! Stealing nice Billy's backy!

But you told me to—

Gag that man.

Well, **that** flopped. Captain, Billy Budd is a French spy.

How widiculous! He hasn't the bwains. Why are you twying to wuin him?

Don't know! Something pederastic, I shouldn't wonder.

Claggart was then constwained to confwont Billy with his baseless accusation, and the outwaged seaman thwew a wight cwoss.

G-g-g-g—

Oh, Chwist.

I'm afwaid he's dead, Budd. You must be uncommonly stwong.

S-save me, c-captain!

Budd was found guilty, and hanged.

G-g-god b-bless you, s-s-sir. G-g-glug.

The wighteousness of the lad! One begins to sympathise with Claggart.

But **I** could have wescued him. Was I wight or wong?

I was wight, as always.

Neddy! Come and eat your stwained cawwots.

MOWAL: Speak cowwectly.

The Widow's Pique

HAVING MORTALLY WOUNDED HIS ADVERSARY, SIR OWEIN PURSUED HIM TO THE GATE OF THE CITY WHEREIN HE (THE ADVERSARY) DWELT.

Come back, Sir Adversary, that I may finish the job!

No, thank you — I have been killed enough for one day.

BUT THE PORTCULLIS CAME DOWN AND SEVERED SIR OWEIN'S HORSE.

Whew! That was close.

CLANG

Almost *too* close.

By my troth, lady, you are the fairest creature on whom I have ever clapped eyes!

Yes, I know, but wear this ring of invisibility and follow me.

If the people of this city found you, they would do away with you unceremoniously.

Unceremoniously? How humiliating.

LUNED, FOR SUCH WAS THE MAIDEN'S NAME, FED AND WASHED SIR OWEIN ALL DAY. NEVER HAD HE BEEN SO FULL, OR SO CLEAN.

WEEP

What means this outcry, Luned?

That is the countess, whose husband you have rubbed out.

WAIL

By my troth, Luned, she is the fairest creature who ever— in short, I love her.

How many troths have you got?

DESPITE HER DISAPPOINTMENT IN SIR OWEIN, LUNED WENT A-WOOING IN HIS BEHALF.

Condolences, Countess! Have I got a man for you···

I am still grieving! How can you be so insensitive? Where? (Weep, wail.)

King Arthur's court! Give me two weeks.

I think you are disgusting, and please step on it.

LUNED AND OWEIN REMAINED IN THE FORMER'S PAD UNTIL IT WAS TIME FOR HIM TO BE PRESENTED TO THE COUNTESS.

I do wish you had a complete horse.

So do I, dear madam, I assure you.

Here he is!

Where?

Make yourself visible, dummy.

This man is too clean! I see it all···

You are right, Countess: it was I who obliterated your spouse. That means I am the better man. Specially now.

Your logic is unassailable.

You may well ask what *I* get out of all this.

MORAL: Have you a troth? Then find someone with a plight.

The Spanner

A poor, ugly, unmarried fisherman awoke one night from a deep dream of peace.

MORAL: May your tribe increase, if you insist.

INCIDENTS IN THE CAREER OF

ELISHA,

MAN OF GOD

ONE DAY HE WAS OPPRESSED BY A FLOCK OF SMALL CHILDREN.

Look at the bald prophet!

If thou art so holy, how come thou hast no hair?

Why wearest thou not a rug?

Behold, this is bloody intolerable.

I curse you in the name of the LORD! 3 bears will tear you unto shreds!

A bit extreme! I have to back him up, but make it 2 bears.

THE BEARS OF THE LORD

AND IT FELL ON ANOTHER DAY THAT A SHUNAMMITE WOMAN CONSTRAINED HIM TO EAT BREAD.

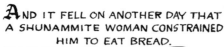

Banana pumpernickel, it melteth in thy mouth.

Banana pumpernickel, how atrocious — but I shall force myself for the LORD's sake.

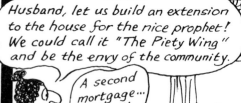

Husband, let us build an extension to the house for the nice prophet! We could call it "The Piety Wing" and be the envy of the community.

A second mortgage... oh well, behold, it is only money.

IN THE PIETY WING

Behold, this is very comfy, Mrs! Is there aught I can do for thee?

Verily, holy man, we are in need of a miracle.

My husband seemeth to lack spermatozoa.

Howbeit, thou shalt conceive.

Nay, my lord, do not lie unto thine handmaid (me).

Unto? I am thinking of **with**.

THE KING OF SYRIA SENT HIS ARMY AGAINST ISRAEL. HE PARTICULARLY HOPED TO CAPTURE ELISHA.

It's a long way to Khafsat al-Kabirah...

LORD, smite them with blindness!

Excuse us, sir, but it is suddenly very dark. Couldst thou direct us to Elisha?

Certainly! Follow me.

HE LED THEM TO THE PLACE WHERE THE ARMY OF ISRAEL WAS ENCAMPED, AND THEY WERE SOON PERSUADED TO GO HOME.

Then there was the time I made an axe-head float. Of course, I was assisted by the LORD.

He is a truly great assistant.

AND THE MANNER IN WHICH ELISHA TRANSFERRED LEPROSY FROM ONE MAN'S NOSE TO ANOTHER'S, IS IT NOT WRITTEN IN THE CHRONICLES OF THE FUNNY PROPHETS?

IN THE YEAR AFTER ELISHA'S DEATH, A CORPSE WAS THROWN INTO HIS SEPULCHRE AND, UPON CONTACT WITH THE HOLY BONES, REVIVED AND WALKED AWAY. *

ELISHA

MORAL: Behold, it ain't what thou knowest but **who** thou knowest.

* **B**UT ELISHA CONTINUED TO BE DEAD.

20

AAGE (pronounced OH-UH) DEFIED HIS FATHER LAST NIGHT BY ATTENDING A

Masquerade

AND FALLING IN LOVE.

Irresponsible, I call it! This is a respectable family! We fall in love with money, not—ugh—people. Go to your room.

What room?

True—I confiscated your room for some previous infraction. Moreover, you are promised to the daughter of Mr Bjornborg the banker.

She probably looks like a standing order.

A VISIT FROM THE BANKER

My daughter is like that too, Batterup. Young people! I can hardly wait until they all get old and feeble.

Absolutely, Bjornborg! A little sciatica is what they need.

Running to masquerades, indeed! In the old days, everybody was in bed by 8 p.m.

8 p.m.? I remember when everybody was sound asleep by 3 p.m.!

In my grandfather's day, nobody ever got up at all!

Right on!

THE TWO MEN ARE HAVING SUCH A GREAT TIME THAT THEY ARE UNAWARE OF AAGE'S DEPARTURE.

HE HAS SNEAKED OFF AGAIN TO THE MASQUERADE WITH—OF ALL PEOPLE—HIS MOTHER!

I know your father is strict, Aage, but beneath that stuffed shirt is a stuffed undershirt.

THE LOVERS MEET AGAIN.

*

*

* Honeyed dialogue omitted out of consideration for the queasy.

SUDDENLY SUSPECTING A RECURRENCE OF FILIAL DISOBEDIENCE, THE FATHERS TURN UP AT THE FESTIVITIES.

The stinkers are in here somewhere.

Would you care to prance, madam?

*

*

Where the @!?⊕£ are they?

IT IS NOW MIDNIGHT! MASKS OFF!

*H.d.o.o.o.c.f.t.q.

Oh—uh...

What a lovely name! I'm Bibi.

Granddad!

My wife!

Yes, I plan to run off with Mr Bjornborg the banker.

It's not love, my dear fellow—merely lust. I hope this won't affect our business arrangements.

MORAL: Unfamiliarity breeds an undeserved lack of contempt.

AUTUMN 79 AD: VESUVIUS HAD JUST ERUPTED; YET THE EMPEROR

TITUS

WAS CASTING ABOUT FOR A WIFE.

(HE HAD HIS PRIORITIES.)

VITELLIA WAS LOVED BY ODIUS.

ODIUS'S NOBLE SERVICES WERE MUCH IN DEMAND.

OBEDIENTLY ATTEMPTING TO SLAY TITUS, ODIUS MISTAKENLY STABBED A LOOK-ALIKE.

TITUS AND VITELLIA AND HIS OTHER WIFE ENJOYED A MÉNAGE À TROIS UNTIL HIS DEATH.

MORAL: Benevolent despotism is in the eye of the beholder. See an ophthalmologist.

TROUBLE FLARED UP AT THE FAG WORKS AS

Carmen

PLUNGED HER STILETTO HEEL INTO ANOTHER EMPLOYEE.

The first thing

EDWARD THE CONFESSOR

did as king was to send his mother into exile.

MORAL: In for a penance, in for a pound.

KING CANUTE (or KNIG CNUT)

refused to meet his rival in single combat to determine which should rule the country.

MORAL: No one can stop flattery at its flood.

The dream of Seamus

One hot afternoon he was digging baked potatoes when along came the master & they fell to talking about dreams.

MORAL: sleep knits up the pale cast of thought.

MORAL: Beware of sharp practices. Also dull ones.

1. Good King Wenceslas

look'd out
On the Feast of Stephen;
Horrid snow lay round about:
Winter getting even.

Repulsively revolting.

Brightly shone the moon that night
Like a phony jewel,
When a poor man claim'd his right
To collect some fu-uel.

Hi there, Your Majesty.

A tugg'd forelock would not go amiss at this juncture.

2. "Hither, page, and tell me now,
In thy stamm'ring fashion:
Who is he, and who art thou?
Why this gath'ring passion?"

Well, I am call'd—

Bah! Many are call'd, but few are frozen. Get on with it.

"Lord, he's but a gelid mass,
Lacking coal and wood, sir;

Impoverish'd as I am, I ain't even got a forelock.

Neither hath he oil nor gas:
That is not so goo-ood, sir."

For whom?

For him.

"Him"? This is an absolute monarchy. No one is real except the king.

3. Icicles on fir and pine
Hung like Woolworth's tinsel:

But where are the bulbs and balls?

And the tasteless prezzies?

"Bring me flesh, and bring me wine,
Bring a sharpen'd pencil.

Letting people have things free
Is not to my liking;

We do not run a welfare state here.

Thou canst say that again.

Chop me down yon cedar tree,
Then prepare for hi-iking."

Do I hear woodpeckers?

No, sire. My teeth are chattering.

How irresponsible.

28

4. Forth like Starsky and like Hutch,
Off they went together,
One attir'd in nothing much,
One in furs and leather.

Soon they reach'd the humble pad,
Shouted through the wall, so:

"Open up thy portal, dad,
And thy wallet a-also."

5. Back they trudg'd through snowy woods:
"Master, that was funny,

How the poor man bought thy goods
When he had no money."

"Credit cards make sales a breeze—
Try to be more clever!
Thanks to 'Charge-a-Christmas', he's
In my debt fore-ever."

6. Early the succeeding morn
Wenceslas woke crownless,

Naked as when he was born,
Slipperless and gownless.

To his page the king was brought:
"Thou thyself hast said it!
In the dead of night I bought
Everything on cre-edit."

Moral: Bar humbug.

29

THE PEBBLE OF TRUTH

THERE ONCE LIVED A KING OF AVERAGE SLEAZINESS, WHO RODE ONE DAY WITH HIS TWIN SONS TO VISIT A KING OF OVERWEENING VANITY.

THE PRINCESS HAD ALREADY BEEN FOUND.

THE LADS' FATHER PREFERRED CASPER, THE YOUNGER AND LESS IDENTICAL OF THE TWINS.

MEANWHILE:

BACK IN AVERAGE SLEAZINESS:

IT WAS, HOWEVER, ONLY A SPHEROID COATED WITH QUICKSILVER; IN SHORT, A MIRROR.

BACK IN OVERWEENING VANITY:

YEARS LATER:

JASPER THEN TRAINED THE TRUTHFUL TOUCHSTONE ON THE FAIR OPHIDIA.

MORAL: Better late, **and** never.

30

Horatio and Emma

or, The Frail Hero

THE NILE: DESTRUCTION OF NAPOLEON'S NAVY

NAPLES: FORTUNE-TELLING AT THE HAMILTONS'

LONDON: CONFRONTATION AT THE NELSONS'

COPENHAGEN: THE FAMOUS TELESCOPE INCIDENT

MERTON

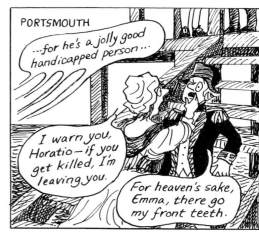

PORTSMOUTH

TRAFALGAR: REDESTRUCTION OF NAPOLEON'S NAVY

MORAL: Only the brave can stand the fair.

The Story of the ENVIOUS MAN
and of him who was envied

IN A TOWN OF NO INCONSIDERABLE UNIMPORTANCE LIVED TWO NEIGHBOURS, ONE OF WHOM MADLY ENVIED THE OTHER.

Here, Ghotbzadeh! Good doggy.

His mutt comes for nothing! Mine doesn't even show up to be fed.

Good morning, neighbour.

Don't "good morning" me, you sanctimonious swine! How come my roof leaks and yours doesn't?

I shall repair your roof.

You do and I'll kill you.

I cannot understand such hostility, can you, puppy wuppy? There is nothing for it but to sell up and depart.

That's right, coward — split! Can't even take a little neighbourly abuse!

FOR SALE

He'll probably get a better price than I could get.

THE GOOD MAN MOVED TO THE CAPITAL, WHERE HE SET UP SHOP AS A DERVISH.

Could you do me a prayer?

Certainly. What would you like?

Rain.

I'd like a dry spell, please.

Right, that's one rain, one dry spell.

REPORTS OF HIS SUCCESS REACHED THE ENVIOUS MAN.

What's he trying to do — torture me?

I will go to the capital, disguised as a suppliant, and then —

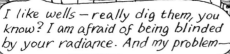

Why do you insist on standing by the well, friend? Why do you cover your face? What is your problem?

I like wells — really dig them, you know? I am afraid of being blinded by your radiance. And my problem—

— is **you**! And now I've solved it.

BUT THE DERVISH WAS SAVED BY BENEVOLENT SPIRITS WHO DWELT IN THE WELL.

Tomorrow, Dervish, the Sultan will come to you with his daughter.

She is possessed by a wicked genie.

You can cure her as follows···

NEXT DAY

You seem a very wet dervish indeed.

Yes, one spent the night in a well. And this is the lovely Princess? Fishface, Fishface, whoopity poo, banish a genie, foo foo foo.

Kh!

I'm **cured**! — and with inches added to my bust.

Fantastic! You really know your stuff.

All in the day's work.

Be my son-in-law.

IN TIME, THE DERVISH SUCCEEDED TO THE THRONE. HE THEN SENT FOR HIS FORMER NEIGHBOUR.

How come you're the Sultan and I'm not? Go ahead — have me killed.

Not at all, old friend! I am going to give you a large sum of money.

You **are** a vindictive bastard.

MORAL: One must be kind in order to be cruel.

Antonio and Wolfgang

THE STORY SO FAR: IT WAS SOON APPARENT THAT LEOPOLD MOZART HAD SIRED A PRODIGY---

What is **happening** in there?

The foetus is composing a symphony!

A bit too Haydn-esque, however, in my opinion.

UNDER HIS DEVOTED FATHER'S INTOLERANT GUIDANCE, YOUNG WOLFGANG PERFORMED AT ALL THE ROYAL COURTS OF EUROPE.

And now, Your Graces and things, Wolfi will play a duet. One false note, kid, and you go to bed without any supper.

My wonderful papa! Not a trace of permissiveness.

NOW READ ON.

Very well, the job is yours! But if you think your old man was strict, you ain't seen nothing.

You just dare to break wind once...

Constanze, I have broken wind and left the Archbishop's service, I have unsuccessfully wooed your sister, I am abysmally poor, and in short—

Oh, Wolfgang, how romantic! Of **course** I will marry you.

Kapellmeister Salieri, my husband W.A. and I are starving picturesquely, and we thought you might—

Yes, yes, show me the music and get lost.

AN INSPECTION OF THE DIVINE SCORES LED TO A CONFRONTATION BETWEEN THE KAPELLMEISTER AND GOD.

Why **him**? Why not **me**? I pay taxes, I brush my teeth...

Should I feign friendship while sabotaging his career?

Should I poison him?

I take your silence to mean "yes".

This is a little tune from "The Marriage of Figaro", which I hope to write.

PLINKY POM, PLINKY POM, PLINKY PIDDLE IDDLE OM...

Playing music he hasn't composed yet! Roll on, strychnine.

Very nice. Shows promise.

A boy named Beethoven played for me recently. I think he may be a genius.

PLONKITY **PLONK**

That's it! Poison the plonk.

Where does this Beethoven live?

MOZART WAS BURIED IN AN UNMARKED GRAVE.

I unmarked it myself.

SALIERI DIED 34 YEARS LATER, AGAIN CASTIGATING GOD.

... and Schubert eluded me, and Weber, and Rossini ...

Don't you **like** me?

MORAL: Not everybody can be a genius, but everybody can assassinate one.

The Debased Alexandrian

A GROUP OF MONKS WERE FINISHING THEIR FRUGAL SUPPER ON THE BANKS OF THE NILE.

THELONIOUS SLEPT ON IT, BUT THIS ONLY SERVED TO HARDEN HIS RESOLVE.

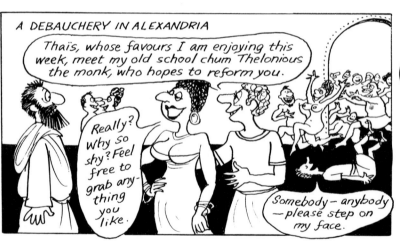

A DEBAUCHERY IN ALEXANDRIA

HOURS LATER

THE NEXT DAY, THAÏS SUFFERED HERSELF TO BE LED TO A CONVENT.

THAT NIGHT, THE MONK HAD A REVELATION.

MORAL: Try not to be too convincing.

Hard Travelling

The children of the Exodus were discontented with their leaders.

THEY WANDERED ON, FIGHTING PERFORCE AGAINST VARIOUS INSENSITIVE PEOPLES.

DEATH OF AARON

RE-DISGRUNTLEMENT OF THE PEOPLE

SERPENTS OF THE LORD, TO BITE THOSE WHO COMPLAIN

ALL THOSE WHO BEHELD THE BRASS SERPENT WERE CURED. *

* BUT THOSE WHO HAD DIED REMAINED DEAD.

MORAL: Hit the road. (Can't hurt! It may emit water.)

35

STAG PARTY

KING ARTHUR AND HIS FRIENDS HAD CAPTURED AND EATEN A STAG, UNTIL THEY WERE NO LONGER HUNGRY AND ONLY THE HEAD REMAINED, WHICH EACH KNIGHT WISHED TO GIVE TO HIS FAVOURITE LADY.

"SINCE THOU ASK," QUOTH GUINEVERE, "HE HAS GONE TO AVENGE SOME FANCIED AFFRONT TO MY QUEENLY PERSON. AND HERE, IN FACT, COMES THE OFFENDER."

ARRIVAL OF GERAINT

ENID WAS POPULAR AT COURT,

AND GERAINT DEVOTED HIMSELF TO TOURNAMENTS, WHICH HE INVARIABLY WON.

BUT ONE DAY, HE WAS SUMMONED TO THE ESTATE OF HIS AGED FATHER.

PATROLLING THE ESTATE

MORAL: Women are what stags are all about.

DURING THE CAPTIVITY (NO, THE OTHER ONE), THREE MEN OF THE BODYGUARD OF KING DARIUS PROPOSED

A DEBATE:

EACH TO ARGUE FOR WHATEVER, IN HIS OPINION, WAS STRONGEST...

... the winner to be given his heart's desire plus clothed in purple plus be called the king's cousin plus drink out of gold goblets plus—

Ye might have consulted **me**.

O king, be our guest! Take credit for this great idea.

WITHIN AN HOUR, THE KING HAD ASSEMBLED ALL THE IMPORTANT MEDES AND PERSIANS.

Distinguished guests, I have had this great idea! Is everybody ready? Then bring in the royal arguers!

MOE'S ARGUMENT

Friends and fellow topers, the strongest thing is **wine**! It maketh us happy, it maketh us blue...

... It causeth grown men to collapse...

... It giveth ush an egzhaggerated shensh of our importansh and abilitiesh...

... and sho, in conclusion, I shimply wish to shay wine ish shtrongesht. Thanksh.

Get off!

JOE'S ARGUMENT

What is strongest? Why, the **king**, of course! He can send us to war, rob us blind with impunity, have us tortured...

... not that **our** enlightened monarch would do such things.

Good thing thou added that, or I would have had thy thumbs dislocated.

ZERUBBABEL'S ARGUMENT

Persons and gentlemen, I give you **women**! They are so strong that the king's floozie putteth his crown on her own head! Behold, she pulleth his beard!

Now let me see some of you **men** try that.

Finally, none of us would be here were it not for our mothers, bless 'em.

I am here in **spite** of my mother.

But strongest of all is **truth**! Behold, truth is stronger than friction!

That soundeth good! Hurrah for truth!

Thou art the winner! That maketh thee my cousin and all that other stuff. What is thy heart's desire?

Same as the truth, O king, which is that thou vowed to rebuild Jerusalem.

Tricked! Kings are not supposed to keep promises! I never suspected he was one of **those**— although he doth have a chosen look about him.

Never mind, sweetie, time for a Zoroastrian cuddle.

MORAL: Talk is not necessarily cheap.

King's' Kids

A witch had kidnapped a princess when the latter was a baby; the latter, in consequence, had never beheld any human except the former.

THE KING OF CRUSTACEA HAD CARELESSLY EXPIRED WITHOUT LEAVING AN HEIR, AND THE PEOPLE HAD SENT THEIR CHIEF FIDDLER IN SEARCH OF A SUITABLE SUCCESSOR.

BUT THE PEOPLE REFUSED TO ACCEPT SUCH RAGAMUFFINS AS HEREDITARY RULERS,

THE ROYAL PAIR WERE DRIVEN FROM THE CITY WITH CONTUMELY,

THE WITCH WAS EXECUTED FOR LYING (ALTHOUGH, FOR THE FIRST TIME IN HER LIFE, SHE HAD TOLD THE TRUTH), AND THE FIDDLER WAS DEPRIVED OF HIS FIDDLE.

MORAL: A sweet disorder in the dress won't get you to the throne room.

The Rape of Lucretia and Subsequent Events

TO SETTLE A WAGER, SEVERAL ROMAN OFFICERS STOLE HOME ONE NIGHT TO CHECK ON THEIR WIVES.

Great Jupiter! How ironic!

That man was rejected by the army as unfit for service.

So it seems that Smuggus here is our only uncuckolded officer! Gentlemen, a toast to the chaste Lucretia!

To the chased Lucretia! Grrr.

THE SPEAKER WAS ETRUSCAN BACHELOR LASCIVIUS SEXTUS, SON OF THE EMPEROR AND GENERAL OF THE ARMY.

And who but my royal self should adorn the noble Smuggus with a nice set of horns?

Bianca, see who is at the door.

Whoever it is knocks very imperially.

RAP BLOODY RAP

Forgive me, dear lady, but my horse is stricken with encephalitis and I crave a night's lodging.

But certainly, Prince! Stand back while I make deep obeisance.

LATER THAT NIGHT

Why, Prince! Do you bring news of my husband?

Yes, and of your "ivory globes circled in blue," as the bard has it.

But I already know about them.

Jibbety jabbity boo! That is Etruscan for "I love you".

No...

I assure you it is! Look it up — not now, of course.

THE FOLLOWING DAY, LUCRETIA SENT FOR SMUGGUS, HER FATHER, THE NOBLE ACRIMONIUS AND OTHERS.

...And that is what transpired! Now I plunge this dagger between the ivory globes, as the bard has it.

THE ROMANS WERE SO INCENSED THAT THE EMPEROR AND HIS LUSTFUL SON WERE BANISHED.

Idiot! You were given command of the army to make war, not love.

Sorry, daddy.

TO PREVENT THE TYRANTS FROM RETURNING, THE PATRIOT PUGNACIUS VORACIUS HELD OFF THE ENEMY WHILE HIS FELLOW ROMANS DESTROYED THE BRIDGE.

There! Rape that, you bastards.

Wonky squidge! That is Etruscan for "curses".

MORAL: When in Rome, don't.

A Den of Inequity

MORAL: A prophet is not without dinner, save in his own country.

The Inlaid Revenue

MORAL: Thou madest thy teeth, now lie in them.

The Seven Angers of Demeter

FOR A GODDESS, DEMETER IS REMARKABLY SLOW TO TAKE OFFENCE. SHE HAS, SO FAR, LOST HER TEMPER ONLY SEVEN TIMES.

THE FOURTH TIME

Persephone! Where *is* the child? Her cereal is getting cold — and I am, after all, the goddess of cereal.

Persephone!

Etc.

ON THE TENTH DAY OF HER WANDERING, DEMETER WAS ENTERTAINED BY A KING AND QUEEN WHO (HAVING HEARD OF THE INEXHAUSTIBLE SUPPLY) REQUESTED HER SERVICE AS WET-NURSE.

Burp

There! And I did it with a breaking heart. Give me a drink.

THE FIFTH TIME

WHEN THE KING'S ELDER SON MADE A RUDE REMARK ABOUT DEMETER'S DRINKING, HE WAS TRANSFORMED INTO A LIZARD.

Happy Hour, folks, ten percent off on all alcoholic — hey!

But all I *said* was…

Sorry! I will compensate for that by making your baby immortal.

Holding him over the fire, thus…

THE SIXTH TIME

Damn!

Who put grease on my hands?

BUT NOW A WITNESS CAME FORWARD WHO HAD SEEN THE ABDUCTION; AND THIS MAN'S TESTIMONY WAS CORROBORATED BY HELIUS.

Dark cloak, shifty eyes…

Hades! I should have known! Why didn't you say something?

Look, lady, I'm paid to shine and that's *it*.

THE SEVENTH TIME

And you can tell your stinking brother —

Your stinking brother —

— that there will be no crops until he releases Persephone.

PEOPLE STARVED. ERYSICHTHON'S LARDER WAS EMPTY.

You don't believe me? Look, bare shelves.

I'm not fussy. I'll eat the shelves.

AND THE REST IS HISTORY, OR AT LEAST MYTHOLOGY!

WE NOW HAVE SOMETHING CALLED "SPRING", NAMED FOR THE OCCASION WHEN DEMETER OBTAINED HER DAUGHTER'S (CONDITIONAL) FREEDOM.

Everybody's doing it.

Olympian Times

DEMETER SPRINGS PERSEPHONE

Hope Springs Eternal Says Joyful Mum

LATE FLASH

ALICE SPRINGS AUSTRALIA

MORAL: Don't talk to strange men, even when they are your uncle.

43

IN THE YEAR 1698, TWO RUSSIANS NAMED **PETER** WERE WORKING IN THE SHIPYARD OF TINKERSDAM, IN HOLLAND.

I am Peter Ivanovich Pisov.

And I am Peter the Gr— the Groper, so called for my prowess with the oppositskaya sex.

[Aside] Almost gave away my identitsky! I am indeed the Tsar, and I have come here to learn the art of shipbuilding, as yet unknown in Russia.

[Still aside] This likeable chap is obviously a deserter from my military establishment.

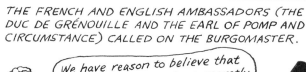

THE FRENCH AND ENGLISH AMBASSADORS (THE DUC DE GRÉNOUILLE AND THE EARL OF POMP AND CIRCUMSTANCE) CALLED ON THE BURGOMASTER.

We have reason to believe that the Russian ruler is here, secretly learning the art of shipbuilding.

Vous comprenez? A clear threat to French supremacy of the seas.

I beg your batrachian pardon.

Never fear, gentlemen! I will make him reveal himself, or my name isn't Mekmijn Van Illa.

Ahoy, shipyard workers! Which of you is called Peter?

All of us, sir—except for three Jans and a Hieronymus.

Very well, then, how many are foreigners?

All of us, sir!

True, I forgot—Holland is a foreign country.

EVENTUALLY, THE NUMBER OF SUSPECTS WAS REDUCED TO TWO.

One can always tell royalty! Welcome to Tinkersdam, your Little Fathership!

But—

You sly benevolent despot! Would you care to attend a little revelry and perhaps even marry my niece?

But—

AT THE REVELRY

This is the niece to whom I referred. Cute, no? I now pronounce you—

But—

One moment, Van Illa! We want this Peter person arrested, not rewarded.

[Aside] Rewarded, dit-il? She is what the English call the toad in the hole.

THROUGH THE INTERCESSION OF THE RUSSIAN AMBASSADOR, COUNT SHEEPOV, BOTH PETERS WERE RETURNED TO THEIR HOMELAND.

I suppose you will have me imprisoned for deserting from the armsky?

Of course, but you can join the navsky the minute we have one.

'Scuse me, but which of you gents am I married to?

MORAL: There is much to be borne under a wandering Tsar.

THE HAREM OF

Shah Hashish

CONSISTED OF ONLY ONE WOMAN, A DIFFERENT ONE EACH MONTH.

Unlike most potentates, I have them in series rather than in parallel. It is due to my electrical engineering background. (See schematic diagram.)

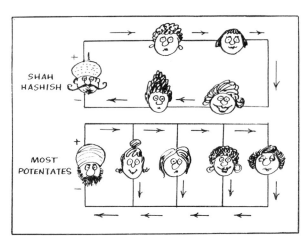

SHAH HASHISH

MOST POTENTATES

THE SHAH NEVER PERMITTED HIMSELF TO BECOME EMOTIONALLY INVOLVED.

Very nice, dear. Your month is up. Goodbye.

I will dispatch an excellent reference to your next owner.

Number 835!

This one is called Magna Qum Louder.

And I quite fancy her myself.

I never bother to remember their tiny names.

He turns me on! It must be his electrical engineering background! By the Most High, I will make him love me before the month is out.

ON THE 29th DAY

What is it with you, O Oligarch of the Tired Blood? I have been positively **sulphurous**, yet your detachment verges on the autistic.

A little to the left. Thank you.

I am more magnetised by this current number than I dare admit! I shall be almost sorry to lose her! Alas, company policy is company policy.

ON THE 31st DAY

I know where the door is, O Secretary.

Not so fast, O Failure! I have a proposition for you.

O mighty Hashish-al-Cannabis-Resin (to give you your full title), here is your newest possession.

Leave it on the bed.

MAGNA SANG, DANCED, ETC. MORE DYNAMICALLY THAN EVER BEFORE.

Frankly, my dear, I give a damn! Who are you?

I am **me**!

By Allah, a noble deception! You have mended my fuse.

ONE YEAR LATER

I have also repaired your socks, O Autocrat of the Perspiring Feet.

Thank you, slave, I mean wife.

Behind the minaret, as usual?

MORAL: Increase voltage and reduce resistance.

To Sleep, Perchance to Stroll

EVERYONE IN THE ALPINE VILLAGE OF QUATSCHENDORF APPROVED THE BETROTHAL OF HEINI AND HEIDI, EXCEPT —

— except **me**, Fräulein Frühstück, proprietress of the inn (colour TV in every room)! I am far from gruntled, and why?

Because he trifled with my affections and then jilted me for this··· this···

Terribly sorry.

It won't happen again.

Oaf! How happy we could have been at the inn (fresh linen daily)!

THE MERRYMAKING WAS INTERRUPTED BY THE ARRIVAL OF A DASHING CAVALIER OF UPPER-CLASS BEARING.

Some sort of nuptials going on, I take it? And you are the bride, my dear? You smell like cheese.

In this country that is the highest compliment one can pay a woman! I am jealous!

Serves you right, jerk.

Sir, will you condescend to spend the night at the inn (tea served in room if desired)?

You are not very incognito! Everyone knows that you are the aristocratic swinger, Count Basle.

Am I? Then cancel the tea. I shall have the proprietress instead.

Oh, sir! Giggle giggle.

Zxk.

But soft! Here comes the bride.

How fortuitous.

Let us tactfully withdraw.

THE INNKEEPER SOON RETURNED WITH THE BRIDEGROOM.

Your fiancée, clodhopper, on the Count's bed! What do you say to that?

Qhpf.

Holy chocolate···

Hello! Where am I? What time is it?

Time to break the engagement, hussy!

Here is your ring! Give me back my dowry!

THE FOLLOWING THURSDAY

Look here, old chap, the girl is obviously a somnambulist.

Indeed? She was brought up as a Lutheran.

And here she comes, risking limb and life.

Ah, why does my beloved Heini hold me responsible for the subconscious motivations of my nocturnal peregrinations? Khpx, gshbzh.

The human mind is a strange thing, Heidi, and so is yours! Forgive me.

What time is it?

Bah! Back to the inn (checkout time strictly enforced).

MORAL: Don't just walk. Talk.

Tripping hither, tripping thither

47

The Novice

FERNANDO, A RECENT MONASTIC RECRUIT, CONFESSED TO HIS FATHER SUPERIOR:

Having exchanged amorous glances with a beautiful virgin, in all conscience I must abandon my intention of becoming a nun.

Go with God, my boy! Or without, as the case may be.

FERNANDO DID NOT KNOW THAT HIS BELOVED LEONORA WAS THE KING'S MISTRESS.

I have had you brought to my magnificent estate, dear one, to tell you that our love is hopeless.

Take this scroll as a consolation prize.

But why? I assure you, my angel, I can easily adapt myself to your great wealth.

A commission in the army! I see! I am to make myself worthy of her by doing heroic deeds.

A piece of cake.

THE KING'S LIAISON WITH LEONORA, KNOWN TO EVERYONE IN SPAIN EXCEPT FERNANDO, HAD GOT HIM INTO DIFFICULTIES WITH THE CHURCH.

In short, His Papacy will interdict you unless you give up this lady and restore your legitimate wife to her rights.

But that is no **fun**! Kings are supposed to have **fun**.

Well, what is it? Can't you see I am busy being excommunicated?

A military hero to see you, Sire.

Ah, Colonel Fernando! The entire country is grateful for your victory over the heathen Moors.

It was a doddle, Majesty, due to my religious upbringing. Name your reward.

My reward? To wed this blessed virgin, Leonora!

This what, who?

Hee! Hee! Ha! Ha! Ho! Ho!

Yes, why not? It will get the Church off my back, and I can still visit her on Thursdays.

FERNANDO WAS FORTHWITH CREATED MARQUÉS DE ESTUPIDEZ.

Dear Fernando, It is time you learned the truth! The fact is that I...

ALAS, THIS LETTER WAS MISLAID AT THE SORTING OFFICE.

AFTER THE WEDDING

Thank you again, Marqués! I trust you will find that I left her in very good condition.

What? So I have been duped!

Oh, dear! My letter must have been mislaid at the sorting office.

FERNANDO FLED BACK TO THE MONASTERY.

Take me back, Father Superior! I am no match for the world's wickedness.

Of course, my son.

Fernando, wait! Let me explain!

LEONORA EXPLAINED.

I am leaving again! Who can account for a mislaid epistle? It is an act of God.

What contributions you might have made to postal theology.

MORAL: Ye shall know the truth, and the truth shall freak you out.

48

The Hedgehog

CHALLENGED THE HARE TO A RACE ACROSS A PLOUGHED FIELD.

MORAL: Married hedgehogs are unscrupulous.

The Nightingale

ADMIRED THE PEACOCKS' EASY VULGARITY...

MORAL: You can probably make a sow's ear out of a silk purse. But please don't.

49

TURNING THE TABLES

Queen Vashti refused to allow her drunken husband to display her before his drunken guests.

Brute! As if I were a prize cow!

For this defiance, I shall procure for myself a **new** prize cow, or my name is not Xerxes or Artaxerxes.

IN THE SAME CAPITAL — SUSA, CITY OF MARCHES — LIVED A FAIR MAIDEN WITH HER KINSMAN-CUM-GUARDIAN.

Listen to this, Esther! "Queen wanted. Mainly decorative. No typing. Experienced virgins only."

Should I apply, cousin Mordecai? LORD knows we need the money.

Yes, but say nothing about being one of the Chosen or thou won't be chosen.

All right, girls, that will be all. Don't call us... Thou! Let me see that tap-dance number again.

And the winner — the envelope, please — is **Esther!**

ONE DAY, MORDECAI OVERHEARD TWO PALACE EUNUCHS PLOTTING AGAINST THE KING.

Thou grab—

And thou stab—

Oho! So gonad removal is no safeguard? A timely word unto my ward-cum-cousin-cum-queen...

THE EUNUCHS WERE HANGED AND REPRIMANDED, AND MORDECAI WAS REWARDED WITH A POSITION AT COURT. THIS ANNOYED CHIEF-OF-STAFF HAMAN.

Well! If it isn't the macronasal scourge of the disbollocked! How about a little "Hail Haman," Mordy?

Sorry. I hail only archangels, God, taxis and the like.

...and they have all the money and they eat Zoroastrian babies and they kiss their own doorways.

Kiss their own doorways? That is going too far.

THE KING SENT PROPOSALS FOR A FINAL SOLUTION TO SATRAPS AND VASSALS THROUGHOUT HIS EMPIRE.

...and join with me in what I like to think of anachronistically as a holy crusade...

How do we get down, Darius?

How did we get up, Cyrus?

Like it? It is for thee.

But my birthday is not until next week.

ON THIS SITE WILL ARISE A 50-CUBIT ERECTION HAMAN & SONS

THE CONNUBIAL

Jason and Medea

RULED CORINTH FOR TEN YEARS, AND HAD FOURTEEN ROYAL OFFSPRING.

What kind of column is that, dad?

Corinthian, stupid! What else would you expect in Corinth?

Don't call my children stupid, stupid.

They are my children too, or are they? I want a divorce.

The ten-year itch, eh? Who is she?

She?

He, then. Whatever.

"SHE" WAS GLAUCE, DAUGHTER OF THE KING OF THEBES.

Then again, Medea bore me all those children.

It would, like, bore me too.

I won't stand in your way, Jason! See, I have constructed this lovely wedding gown for What's Her Name.

You are an absolute brick, ex-dear.

She made me a dress? The woman is like weird! Think it fits? I'm a 14.

What a coincidence! I have 14 kiddie-winkies.

WHEN GLAUCE TRIED ON THE GIFT, IT BURST INTO FLAMES, CONSUMING ALL THE DISTINGUISHED GUESTS.

What a pity! Jason seems to have survived.

Wait till I get my hands on Medea.

EVEN ZEUS WAS IMPRESSED.

Some kind of slaughter, baby, positively godlike! How about you and me—

No, thanks.

HERA WAS GRATEFUL.

You must be the first mortal who ever turned him down!

Bah.

As a reward, I will make your children immortal. Just follow these simple instructions…

Why are you sacrificing us to Hera, mum?

HERA

For your **souls**, pet! Trust mummy.

WAS THERE EVER A MORE UNSELFISH PARENT? HOW DIFFERENT FROM EURIPIDES' SLANDEROUS VERSION OF THESE EVENTS.

MEDEA FLED, ALWAYS PRECEDED BY HER UNSAVOURY REPUTATION.

THEBES
ATHENS
ANYWHERE

AS FOR JASON, HE BECAME AN ANTIQUATED PEST.

Buy me a drink, friend, and I will tell you again how I captured the golden faeces.

I will buy you one on condition that you **don't**, Landlord! One hemlock on the rocks, with a twist.

MORAL: Mother knows worst.

"Le Chevalier Mal Fait"

BY MEANS OF MAGICAL CHICANERY, FOUR QUEENS CAPTURED, BUT FAILED TO CAPTIVATE, SIR LANCELOT.

What a man! Even his muscles have muscles.

And now, sir, choose! Which of us will you serve?

None, madam! And let me tell you I would bust out of this dungeon, were it not for my exaggerated chivalrous misconceptions.

THAT EVENING A FAIR DAMSEL BROUGHT SIR LANCELOT HIS DINNER.

Devour your bubble and squeak, sir, and I will set you free on one condition.

I suppose you wish to see me flex my pecs?

Only in a good cause, as follows...

My sister is held prisoner by evil Sir Turbine, who desires to ravish her against her will.

Upon my knightly honour, fair damsel, that is the worst kind of ravish.

Sir, are you the ravishing Sir Turbine?

I am indeed he, actually.

Then prepare to defend yourself!

Why? Am I in some danger?

LANCELOT THEN CAME TO A TOWN WHERE HE WAS WELCOMED ENTHUSIASTICALLY.

Just the man we need! In a certain chapel there lurks a dreadful serpent—

—guarding Elaine the fair, who is lying in boiling water.

ADVISING IT TO DEFEND ITSELF, LANCELOT QUICKLY DISPATCHED THE SERPENT.

And there is Elaine the fair, in boiling water! Alas, lady, you must be in amazing discomfort.

Yes, shall we discuss it?

ELAINE TOO HAD RECOURSE TO MAGIC, TRICKING LANCELOT INTO BELIEVING HER TO BE GUINEVERE.

Woe is I! I have been unfaithful to my dearest friend's wife! I shall go mad.

AND GO MAD HE DID, FOR A YEAR AND A DAY.

Let me make it quite clear, gentlemen! A free economy is the best mechanism for slowing population growth! But as for coercive family planning...

Year and a day are up. Time to be sane.

IN SELF-IMPOSED EXILE, UNDER AN ASSUMED NAME, LANCELOT CHALLENGED ALL COMERS TO JOUST FOR THE HONOUR OF THEIR LADIES.

You win, sir! My lady has lost her honour! Your name?

Le Chevalier Mal Fait! That means "The Depraved Knight".

I beg to differ! It means "The Badly Made Horseperson".

Sir Lancelot! I have been sent to seek you and bring you back to Camelot for your sins...

...which are due for renewal, you lucky horseperson.

MORAL: Live up to your bad name.

FISHY BITS

THE PATRIARCH TOBIT OFTEN SEARCHED THE STREETS OF NINEVEH FOR BODIES, WHICH HE PIOUSLY BURIED.

Art thou of the Hebrew faith, dead friend? Really? Which tribe?

RETURNING ONE NIGHT FROM THIS HOLY CHORE···

Wife! Wife! As I lay down in the garden for a kip I was pelted with sparrow dung!

Tobit, thou shlimazl, how many times have I proclaimed "Never sleep with the eyes ajar"? But who listeneth?

O LORD, I have been blinded by sparrows, as thou probably knowest! Howbeit I should like to see my son Tobias marry a nice girl, preferably a relative.

But our only relative is cousin Sara, the minx with the jinx.

POSSESSED BY A JEALOUS DEMON, SARA HAD BEEN WIDOWED SEVEN TIMES ON AS MANY WEDDING NIGHTS.

O LORD, thou shouldst hear what the neighbours say about me!

Furthermore, I am getting fat. The demon eateth like a horse.

I DO NOT.

I have a couple of prayers here, Archangel Raphael, and I am minded to respond in my own funny way. Deal with them, wilt thou?

Yes, **sir**!

Come along, Tobias! We are off to the town where thy cousin Sara liveth.

Are we aviating? For I perceive thou art equipped with alate appendages.

THAT EVENING, AS TOBIAS WASHED AT THE RIVER, A FISH LEAPED OUT OF THE WATER AS IF TO DEVOUR HIM.

Oy

Fear not! **We** will devour **it** — after extracting certain organs.

AT SARA'S

But, cousin, what about the jinx?

Eighth time lucky, cousin! My winged friend hath taught me a trick with a fish liver···

NO! PLEASE! NOT THE FISH LIVER TRICK!

WHEN THE LIVER HAD BEEN IGNITED AND THE APPROPRIATE INCANTATIONS SPOKEN, THE EVIL SPIRIT FLED FROM THE WOMAN EVEN UNTO LIBYA, WHERE IT CAN STILL BE FOUND.

I SHALL TRANSFORM MYSELF INTO A FEEBLE-MINDED COLONEL.

Here cometh our son, with cousin Sara and some kind of bird.

I have **had it** with birds.

FOLLOWING INSTRUCTIONS, TOBIAS APPLIED THE FISH'S GALL BLADDER TO HIS FATHER'S EYES AND RESTORED HIS SIGHT.

Sir, thou hast done wonders for this family! How much do we owe thee?

On the house, folks. Plenty of mansions.

MORAL:
In the heavenly cookbook are many seafood recipes.

Kätthe, a simple peasant lass, often invoked the

FOREST SPIRITS,

relying on their anthropomorphic benevolence.

THE FOLLOWING DAY, AS THE VILLAGERS PRANCED ABOUT IN BRAINLESS CELEBRATION OF THE MARRIAGE, GERHART EMERGED FROM THE FOREST.

LATER, ALONE IN THE FOREST, GERHART WAS SUDDENLY ACCOSTED.

ENRAGED AT BEING TOLD TO PEE OFF IN THE PRESENCE OF A PLEBEIAN, THE COUNT RECKLESSLY SPURRED HIS HORSE AND WAS SOON THROWN.

55

IDAMANTE, REGENT OF CRETE, LOVED THE CAPTIVE TROJAN PRINCESS ILIA, AND WAS LOVED BY THE REFUGEE ELECTRA.

See, dearest, I have removed your chains! Vouchsafe me a kiss.

Never!

I love him too, but he is a hated Greek of some sort.

What's she got that I ain't, aside from beauty and brains?

BUT EVEN AS HE DECLARED HIS LOVE, HIS FATHER, KING

IDOMENEO,

WAS CAUGHT IN A VIOLENT TEMPEST.

Neptune, spare me! In return I will, um, sacrifice the first person I meet upon disembarking.

AGREED! LET'S SEE, HOW DO YOU TURN THIS THING OFF?

Daddy! You're safe! How was the war?

Help! I have vowed to expunge my own son!

Out of my sight, nitwit!

Why is he so mean? I bet he hates me just because I grew up to be a soprano.

THE KING CONSULTED HIS TRUSTED FRIEND.

...so that's the story, trusted friend! I made this rash promise. Now how can I weasel out of it?

Send him away! The gods have shockingly short memories, you know. And send Electra with him — she depresses everyone with her talk about how mourning becomes her.

Well, lover boy, you and I are going on a little trippy poo.

What have I done to deserve this?

Like my new grief outfit?

BUT THEY WERE UNABLE TO SAIL! THE FURIOUS NEPTUNE SENT MOUN-TAINOUS WAVES THAT ENGULFED THE TOWN, DROWNING MANY INNOCENT CITIZENS.

BREACH OF CONTRACT! I SHOULD KNOW BETTER THAN TO TRUST MORTALS— BUT THAT'S ME EVERY TIME, A PUSHOVER.

I am off to do battle! By the way, Ilia, I still love you.

And I you! Under the circumstances, I can no longer withhold this information.

THE YOUTH RETURNED VICTORIOUS FROM THE FLOOD, JUST AS HIS FATHER HAD MADE A FULL AND FRANK PUBLIC CONFESSION.

Whew! Soaked but happy...

And now I have to sacrifice him, folks. Ah, Idamante! Look, I'm awfully sorry, but —

HOWEVER, NEPTUNE RELENTED, UPON ONE CONDITION:

THAT YOU STEP DOWN IN FAVOUR OF YOUR SON! HE IS MORE HONOURABLE THAN YOU, AS WHO ISN'T?

But he is a soprano.

CRETAN! ASK ZEUS TO MAKE HIM A BARITONE.

Hel-lo there.

I don't know— your previous voice made me feel more motherly.

You people know what I did to **my** mother?

Now, now.

MORAL:
When you risk a life, make sure it is that of a total stranger.

56

WHOLLY WAR

TANCREDI, A CRUSADER, HAD FALLEN IN LOVE WITH THE SARACEN MAIDEN CLORINDA.

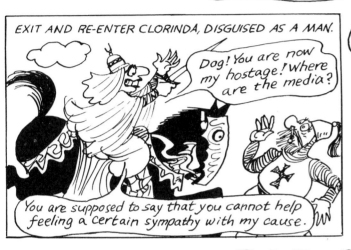

MORAL: Heterosexual homicide is forbidden (except in the Koran).

* TRANSLATED INTO ANCIENT GREEK FROM THE ORIGINAL EQUINE

IT WAS AS A YOUNG MEDICAL STUDENT THAT

Galileo

FIRST ANTAGONISED THE CHURCH. HE NOTICED A LAMP SWINGING IN THE CATHEDRAL, AND---

IT IS AN ANCIENT MARINER

AND HE STOPPETH ONE OF THREE.

"ONE AUTUMN DAY WE SAILED AWAY;
WE THOUGHT 'TWAS SPRING," QUOTH HE.
"NO LEAVES WERE TURNING COLOUR, FOR
I'D CUT DOWN EVERY TREE,
DESTROYING THE ENVIRONMENT
BEFORE I PUT TO SEA.

THE SAILORS' BANE, DYSLEXIA,
HAD CAST ON US ITS BLIGHT:
THE SUN CAME UP UPON THE LEFT,
OR POSSIBLY THE RIGHT;
AND SOUTH OR NORTH AND BACK OR FORTH
WE HASTENED DAY AND NIGHT.

AND THEN AN ACID RAIN DID COME
TO BITE HOLES IN MY NECK:
I SPRANG ASIDE AND WATCHED IT EAT
ITS WAY INTO THE DECK!
TO THE ORDER OF 'ECOLOGY'
I WROTE A MENTAL CHEQUE."

"I FEAR THEE, ANCIENT MARINER!"
"BELT UP, THOU WEDDING-GUEST!
FOR AS WE CURSED, THE STORM DISPERSED
AS THOUGH AT THE BEHEST
OF DOLPHINS SWIMMING TO THE EAST—
I TELL A LIE, 'TWAS WEST.

THEY LEAPED AND GRINNED LIKE IDIOTS
AND SMOOTHLY WE DID SAIL—"
"O MARINER, THOU SHOTST A FISH!"
"THOU INTERRUPTST MY TALE;
I DID NOT SHOOT THE PORPOISE CUTE:
I SHOT, INSTEAD, A WHALE.

AND NOW THE SKY GREW VERY DARK
AND RAPIDLY THERE CAME
A RADIOACTIVE FALLOUT FROM
SOME MILITARY GAME,
AND EVERYBODY'S BEARD FELL OFF,
AND I WAS HELD TO BLAME.

A GROUP OF SHIPMATES CLUSTERED ROUND,
A LARGE AND MENACING BEVY:
'THINKST THOU CETACEANS GROW ON TREES?
A PENANCE WE WILL LEVY!'
THEY MADE ME WEAR THE FLIPPING WHALE,
AND IT WAS BLOODY HEAVY.

THE WIND DIED DOWN, OUR SPIRITS
    DROOPED;
WHO COULD A DRINK REFUSE?
AND SOON OUR SPIRITS WERE ALL
    GONE,
AS VOID AS LAST WEEK'S NEWS;
WATER, WATER, EVERYWHERE,
NOR ANY DROP OF BOOZE.

BUT LO! A PHANTOM SHIP APPEARS
ALTHOUGH THERE'S NOT A BREEZE;
IS THAT A WOMAN CASTING DICE
WITH DEATH? HAVE I D.T.'S?
AND 'HELLO, SAILOR!' SHE EXCLAIMS,
'I'VE WON THY SOUL. SAY CHEESE!'

MY SHIPMATES ALL DROP DEAD AT ONCE,
AS IF THEY'D BEEN REHEARSED;
ALONE, ALONE, ALL, ALL ALONE! —
BUT THAT WAS NOT THE WORST —
(AND COULDST THOU SPARE SOME
CASH? THIS TALK
IS GIVING ME A THIRST.)

THEN EVERY THREATENED SPECIES CAME
AND SWAM BESIDE THE SHIP,
AND GAZED AT ME REPROACHFULLY:
A PSYCHEDELIC TRIP — "
"WHAT! TAK'ST THOU DRUGS, O
MARINER?"
"PRAY BUTTON, SIR, THY LIP.

FOR HAD I NOT CHOPPED DOWN
THE TREES,
AND POISONED ALL THE SOIL?
THOSE CREATURES HAD TO LEARN
TO SWIM,
AND IT WAS FEARFUL TOIL;
AND NOW A MIGHTY TANKER CAME
AND SPILLED ITS LOAD OF OIL.

THE LAND-BASED CREATURES QUICKLY
SANK
TO THEIR ETERNAL PEACE,
WHILST I, POOR BUGGER, STOOD ON DECK
AWAITING MY RELEASE,
AND NEXT A MESS OF FISH AROSE,
SMELLING LIKE AXLE-GREASE.

I CRAWLED INTO MY BUNK AND HAD
A REVERIE OF A SORT:
I DREAMT A SPIRIT SPAKE TO ME
AND OFFERED ME A QUART.
MY BUNK WAS ON THE STARBOARD
SIDE —
NO, HANG ABOUT, 'TWAS PORT.

AND THIS WAS WHAT THE SPIRIT SAID:
'THOU LIKELY FIND'ST IT ODD
THAT ALL BUT THEE WERE MASSACRED,
BUT THAT'S THE WAY WITH GOD;
HE'LL WRECK THE JOINT TO MAKE
HIS POINT —
THOU DIG'ST? I SEE THEE NOD.

ALL FORMS OF LIFE,' THE SPIRIT SAID,
'ARE SACRED IN HIS EYES;
HE SLAYETH THEM HIMSELF, OF COURSE,
BUT THEN HE'S AWFULLY WISE' —
AND THEN WAS GONE ERE I COULD
ASK
THE RULE ON SWATTING FLIES.

THOU LISTENED TO MY NARRATIVE:
THOU'RT BETTER THAN A SHRINK!
IT'S CALLED AN AUTUMN TALE
BECAUSE
IT AUTUMN MAKE YOU THINK."
"I FEAR THY PUNS, VILE MARINER!"
"BAH! HOW ABOUT THAT DRINK?"

Incident in Palestine

A LONE CRUSADER MADE HIS WAY ALONG THE SHORES OF THE DEAD SEA, LOST IN WHAT HE BELIEVED TO BE THOUGHT.

THE SARACEN RODE RAPIDLY ROUND AND ROUND THE KNIGHT...

...WHO, GROWING DIZZY, FLUNG A MISSILE, OR MISSAL, AT HIS ADVERSARY.

QUICKLY REMOUNTING, THE EASTERN CAVALIER RESUMED HIS ORBIT, FROM WHICH HE FIRED MANY ARROWS.

THE EUROPEAN WAS ONLY FEIGNING DEATH, AND QUICKLY OVERCAME HIS UNPREPARED FOE.

MORAL: None are so disarmingly peace-loving as the disarmed.